A Book Tracking Journal

For Ladies Who Love to Read

Book 1

Susan A. Jennings

For more books, novels, journals and colouring books
Website: www.susanajennings.com
Email: susan@susanajennings.com

ISBN: 978-0-9937433-7-5

This Book
Tracking
Journal

Belongs to....

Name: _____

Contact: _____

Dedication

To All
reader and author friends
around the world.
For the words written and read
and stories told
I dedicate
this book to you

Introduction

I am an avid reader and don't feel it necassary to banish a novel or most books, once read, especially if it has given me many hours of pleasure. Perhaps it is the author in me, knowing how many hours goes into writing a book. The exception would be passing it on to another reader or donating to charity sharing the pleasure of reading.

Collecting books is a passion for me, particularly, physical books. I do read e-books but the old fashioned paper takes presidence as I fill up my bookshelves. I have difficulty keeping track of what I have read and not read, enjoyed or not enjoyed. When I find an author I really love I want to read all his or her books. Whether the books are stand alone, part of a series, a lengthy saga or a sequel; keeping tabs on old and new is daunting. I have been know to buy books twice--publishers have a habit of changing book covers.

How do I keep track? I searched for a reader's journal and found many but not quite what I wanted. I decided to make my own journal and share it with readers.

The result, a small neat journal designed by me for you to help you organize your books and reading.

A Book Tracking Journal - For Ladies Who Love to Read

Easy to use:
1. Add the title, author, genre, format and number of pages
2. Name the series and serial number if applicable
3. Note the date you started and finished reading
4. Rate the read 1- 5 by filling in the mini books
5. Jot down the theme or how you felt
6. Tick off whether the story was good, okay or poor
7. Would you recommend this book and to whom?
8. Where did you purchase this book?
9. Where were you when you read this book?
10. List your own personal table of contents

Have fun and enjoy this book tracking joural for ladies!

Table of Contents

Page #   Book Title & Author

Table of Contents

Page #　　　　　　　　Book Title & Author

My Review and Thoughts...

"I decalre after all there is no enjoyment like reading! How much sooner one tires of anything than a book!"

Jane Austen - *Pride and Predjudice*

Title: _____

Subtitle: _____

Author: _____

Genre: _____

Format: Print: ☐   E-book: ☐   # of Pages: _____

Series title: _____ #_____

Next book in series: _____

Date of purchase: _____ Date read: _____

Place of purchase: _____

I read this book: At home: ☐   Away: ☐   In transit: ☐

How would you rate this book?

Fill in mini books below 1 for poor and 5 for excellent

This book made me feel...

Happy: ☐   Sad: ☐   Angry: ☐   Warm: ☐ Disturbed: ☐

Other emotion: _____

Was the story...	Good ☐	Okay ☐	Poor ☐
Quality of writing...	Good ☐	Okay ☐	Poor ☐
Were the Characters...	Good ☐	Okay ☐	Poor ☐
Was the plot engaging...	Good ☐	Okay ☐	Poor ☐
Was it a page turner...	Good ☐	Okay ☐	Poor ☐
Was it enjoyable...	Good ☐	Okay ☐	Poor ☐
Recommend it...	Yes ☐	No ☐	

Friends who might enjoy this book...

Name: _____

My Review and Thoughts...

"Women want love
to be a novel. Men,
a short story."
Daphne du Maurier

Title: _____

Subtitle: _____

Author: _____

Genre: _____

Format: Print: ☐   E-book: ☐   # of Pages: _____

Series title: _____ # _____

Next book in series: _____

Date of purchase: _____ Date read: _____

Place of purchase: _____

I read this book: At home: ☐   Away: ☐   In transit: ☐

How would you rate this book?

Fill in mini books below 1 for poor and 5 for excellent

This book made me feel...

Happy: ☐   Sad: ☐   Angry: ☐   Warm: ☐   Disturbed: ☐

Other emotion: _____

Was the story...	Good ☐	Okay ☐	Poor ☐
Quality of writing...	Good ☐	Okay ☐	Poor ☐
Were the Characters...	Good ☐	Okay ☐	Poor ☐
Was the plot engaging...	Good ☐	Okay ☐	Poor ☐
Was it a page turner...	Good ☐	Okay ☐	Poor ☐
Was it enjoyable...	Good ☐	Okay ☐	Poor ☐
Recommend it...	Yes ☐	No ☐	

Friends who might enjoy this book...

Name: _____

My Review and Thoughts...

"For a moment I was distracted. Books always did that to me...I like the creamy pages, the smell of ink, all the secrets locked inside."

Elizabeth C. Bunce

Title: _____

Subtitle: _____

Author: _____

Genre: _____

Format: Print: ☐   E-book: ☐   # of Pages: _____

Series title: _____ #_____

Next book in series: _____

Date of purchase: _____ Date read: _____

Place of purchase: _____

I read this book: At home: ☐   Away: ☐   In transit: ☐

How would you rate this book?

Fill in mini books below 1 for poor and 5 for excellent

This book made me feel...

Happy: ☐   Sad: ☐   Angry: ☐   Warm: ☐   Disturbed: ☐

Other emotion: _____

Was the story...	Good ☐	Okay ☐	Poor ☐
Quality of writing...	Good ☐	Okay ☐	Poor ☐
Were the Characters...	Good ☐	Okay ☐	Poor ☐
Was the plot engaging...	Good ☐	Okay ☐	Poor ☐
Was it a page turner...	Good ☐	Okay ☐	Poor ☐
Was it enjoyable...	Good ☐	Okay ☐	Poor ☐
Recommend it...	Yes ☐	No ☐	

Friends who might enjoy this book...

Name: _____

My Review and Thoughts...

"I kept always two books in my
pocket, one to read,
one to write in."
Robert Louis
Stevenson

Title: _____

Subtitle: _____

Author: _____

Genre: _____

Format: Print: ☐ E-book: ☐   # of Pages: _____

Series title: _____ #_____

Next book in series: _____

Date of purchase: _____ Date read: _____

Place of purchase: _____

I read this book: At home: ☐ Away: ☐ In transit: ☐

How would you rate this book?

Fill in mini books below 1 for poor and 5 for excellent

This book made me feel...

Happy: ☐ Sad: ☐ Angry: ☐ Warm: ☐ Disturbed: ☐

Other emotion: _____

Was the story...	Good ☐	Okay ☐	Poor ☐
Quality of writing...	Good ☐	Okay ☐	Poor ☐
Were the Characters...	Good ☐	Okay ☐	Poor ☐
Was the plot engaging...	Good ☐	Okay ☐	Poor ☐
Was it a page turner...	Good ☐	Okay ☐	Poor ☐
Was it enjoyable...	Good ☐	Okay ☐	Poor ☐
Recommend it...	Yes ☐	No ☐	

Friends who might enjoy this book...

Name: _____

My Review and Thoughts...

"However, the majority of women are neither harlots nor courtesans;
nor do they sit clasping pug dogs to dusty velvet all
through the summer afternoon."

Virginia Woolf

Title: _____

Subtitle: _____

Author: _____

Genre: _____

Format: Print: ☐ E-book: ☐   # of Pages: _____

Series title: _____ # _____

Next book in series: _____

Date of purchase: _____ Date read: _____

Place of purchase: _____

I read this book: At home: ☐ Away: ☐ In transit: ☐

How would you rate this book?

Fill in mini books below 1 for poor and 5 for excellent

☐ ☐ ☐ ☐ ☐

This book made me feel...

Happy: ☐ Sad: ☐ Angry: ☐ Warm: ☐ Disturbed: ☐

Other emotion: _____

Was the story...	Good ☐	Okay ☐	Poor ☐
Quality of writing...	Good ☐	Okay ☐	Poor ☐
Were the Characters...	Good ☐	Okay ☐	Poor ☐
Was the plot engaging...	Good ☐	Okay ☐	Poor ☐
Was it a page turner...	Good ☐	Okay ☐	Poor ☐
Was it enjoyable...	Good ☐	Okay ☐	Poor ☐
Recommend it...	Yes ☐	No ☐	

Friends who might enjoy this book...

Name: _____

My Review and Thoughts...

"The hard part about writing
a novel is finishing it."
Enrnest
Hemingway

Title: _____

Subtitle: _____

Author: _____

Genre: _____

Format: Print: ☐   E-book: ☐   # of Pages: _____

Series title: _____ #_____

Next book in series: _____

Date of purchase: _____ Date read: _____

Place of purchase: _____

I read this book: At home: ☐   Away: ☐   In transit: ☐

How would you rate this book?
Fill in mini books below 1 for poor and 5 for excellent

This book made me feel...
Happy: ☐   Sad: ☐   Angry: ☐   Warm: ☐ Disturbed: ☐
Other emotion: _____

Was the story...	Good ☐	Okay ☐	Poor ☐
Quality of writing...	Good ☐	Okay ☐	Poor ☐
Were the Characters...	Good ☐	Okay ☐	Poor ☐
Was the plot engaging...	Good ☐	Okay ☐	Poor ☐
Was it a page turner...	Good ☐	Okay ☐	Poor ☐
Was it enjoyable...	Good ☐	Okay ☐	Poor ☐
Recommend it...	Yes ☐	No ☐	

Friends who might enjoy this book...

Name: _____

My Review and Thoughts...

"I am no bird; and no nest ensnares me; I am a free human being with an
independent will."
Charlotte Bronte

Title: _____

Subtitle: _____

Author: _____

Genre: _____

Format: Print: ☐ E-book: ☐   # of Pages: _____

Series title: _____ #_____

Next book in series: _____

Date of purchase: _____ Date read: _____

Place of purchase: _____

I read this book: At home: ☐ Away: ☐ In transit: ☐

How would you rate this book?
Fill in mini books below 1 for poor and 5 for excellent

This book made me feel...
Happy: ☐ Sad: ☐ Angry: ☐ Warm: ☐ Disturbed: ☐
Other emotion: _____

Was the story...	Good ☐	Okay ☐	Poor ☐
Quality of writing...	Good ☐	Okay ☐	Poor ☐
Were the Characters...	Good ☐	Okay ☐	Poor ☐
Was the plot engaging...	Good ☐	Okay ☐	Poor ☐
Was it a page turner...	Good ☐	Okay ☐	Poor ☐
Was it enjoyable...	Good ☐	Okay ☐	Poor ☐
Recommend it...	Yes ☐	No ☐	

Friends who might enjoy this book...

Name: _____

My Review and Thoughts...

"There is no greater agony than
bearing an untold story
inside you."

Maya Angelou

Title: _____

Subtitle: _____

Author: _____

Genre: _____

Format: Print: ☐ E-book: ☐ # of Pages: _____

Series title: _____ # _____

Next book in series: _____

Date of purchase: _____ Date read: _____

Place of purchase: _____

I read this book: At home: ☐ Away: ☐ In transit: ☐

How would you rate this book?

Fill in mini books below 1 for poor and 5 for excellent

This book made me feel...

Happy: ☐ Sad: ☐ Angry: ☐ Warm: ☐ Disturbed: ☐

Other emotion: _____

Was the story...	Good ☐	Okay ☐	Poor ☐
Quality of writing...	Good ☐	Okay ☐	Poor ☐
Were the Characters...	Good ☐	Okay ☐	Poor ☐
Was the plot engaging...	Good ☐	Okay ☐	Poor ☐
Was it a page turner...	Good ☐	Okay ☐	Poor ☐
Was it enjoyable...	Good ☐	Okay ☐	Poor ☐
Recommend it...	Yes ☐	No ☐	

Friends who might enjoy this book...

Name: _____

My Review and Thoughts...

"I've got the key to my castle in the air, but whether I can unlock the door remains to be seen."
Lousia May Alcott

Title: _____

Subtitle: _____

Author: _____

Genre: _____

Format: Print: ☐   E-book: ☐   # of Pages: _____

Series title: _____ #_____

Next book in series: _____

Date of purchase: _____ Date read: _____

Place of purchase: _____

I read this book: At home: ☐   Away: ☐   In transit: ☐

How would you rate this book?
Fill in mini books below 1 for poor and 5 for excellent

This book made me feel...

Happy: ☐ Sad: ☐ Angry: ☐ Warm: ☐ Disturbed: ☐

Other emotion: _____

Was the story...	Good ☐	Okay ☐	Poor ☐
Quality of writing...	Good ☐	Okay ☐	Poor ☐
Were the Characters...	Good ☐	Okay ☐	Poor ☐
Was the plot engaging...	Good ☐	Okay ☐	Poor ☐
Was it a page turner...	Good ☐	Okay ☐	Poor ☐
Was it enjoyable...	Good ☐	Okay ☐	Poor ☐
Recommend it...	Yes ☐	No ☐	

Friends who might enjoy this book...

Name: _____

My Review and Thoughts...

"If a book is well written,
I always find it short."

Jane Austen
Sense & Sensibility

Title: _____

Subtitle: _____

Author: _____

Genre: _____

Format: Print: ☐ E-book: ☐   # of Pages: _____

Series title: _____ # _____

Next book in series: _____

Date of purchase: _____ Date read: _____

Place of purchase: _____

I read this book: At home: ☐ Away: ☐ In transit: ☐

How would you rate this book?

Fill in mini books below 1 for poor and 5 for excellent

This book made me feel...

Happy: ☐ Sad: ☐ Angry: ☐ Warm: ☐ Disturbed: ☐

Other emotion: _____

Was the story...	Good ☐	Okay ☐	Poor ☐
Quality of writing...	Good ☐	Okay ☐	Poor ☐
Were the Characters...	Good ☐	Okay ☐	Poor ☐
Was the plot engaging...	Good ☐	Okay ☐	Poor ☐
Was it a page turner...	Good ☐	Okay ☐	Poor ☐
Was it enjoyable...	Good ☐	Okay ☐	Poor ☐
Recommend it...	Yes ☐	No ☐	

Friends who might enjoy this book...

Name: _____

My Review and Thoughts...

"Whether I'm at the office, at home, or on the road, I always have
a stack of books I'm looking forward to reading."
Bill Gates

Title: _____

Subtitle: _____

Author: _____

Genre: _____

Format: Print: ☐ E-book: ☐   # of Pages: _____

Series title: _____ # _____

Next book in series: _____

Date of purchase: _____ Date read: _____

Place of purchase: _____

I read this book: At home: ☐ Away: ☐ In transit: ☐

How would you rate this book?

Fill in mini books below 1 for poor and 5 for excellent

This book made me feel...

Happy: ☐ Sad: ☐ Angry: ☐ Warm: ☐ Disturbed: ☐

Other emotion: _____

Was the story...	Good ☐	Okay ☐	Poor ☐
Quality of writing...	Good ☐	Okay ☐	Poor ☐
Were the Characters...	Good ☐	Okay ☐	Poor ☐
Was the plot engaging...	Good ☐	Okay ☐	Poor ☐
Was it a page turner...	Good ☐	Okay ☐	Poor ☐
Was it enjoyable...	Good ☐	Okay ☐	Poor ☐
Recommend it...	Yes ☐	No ☐	

Friends who might enjoy this book...

Name: _____

My Review and Thoughts...

"I read for pleasure and that is
the moment I learn the most."

Margaret Atwood

Title: _____

Subtitle: _____

Author: _____

Genre: _____

Format: Print: ☐   E-book: ☐   # of Pages: _____

Series title: _____ #_____

Next book in series: _____

Date of purchase: _____ Date read: _____

Place of purchase: _____

I read this book: At home: ☐   Away: ☐   In transit: ☐

How would you rate this book?

Fill in mini books below 1 for poor and 5 for excellent

This book made me feel...

Happy: ☐   Sad: ☐   Angry: ☐   Warm: ☐   Disturbed: ☐

Other emotion: _____

Was the story...	Good ☐	Okay ☐	Poor ☐
Quality of writing...	Good ☐	Okay ☐	Poor ☐
Were the Characters...	Good ☐	Okay ☐	Poor ☐
Was the plot engaging...	Good ☐	Okay ☐	Poor ☐
Was it a page turner...	Good ☐	Okay ☐	Poor ☐
Was it enjoyable...	Good ☐	Okay ☐	Poor ☐
Recommend it...	Yes ☐	No ☐	

Friends who might enjoy this book...

Name: _____

My Review and Thoughts...

"I only read biographies, metaphysics and psychology. I can dream up my own fiction."

Mae West

Title: _____

Subtitle: _____

Author: _____

Genre: _____

Format: Print: ☐   E-book: ☐   # of Pages: _____

Series title: _____ # _____

Next book in series: _____

Date of purchase: _____ Date read: _____

Place of purchase: _____

I read this book: At home: ☐   Away: ☐   In transit: ☐

How would you rate this book?

Fill in mini books below 1 for poor and 5 for excellent

This book made me feel...

Happy: ☐   Sad: ☐   Angry: ☐   Warm: ☐ Disturbed: ☐

Other emotion: _____

Was the story...	Good ☐	Okay ☐	Poor ☐
Quality of writing...	Good ☐	Okay ☐	Poor ☐
Were the Characters...	Good ☐	Okay ☐	Poor ☐
Was the plot engaging...	Good ☐	Okay ☐	Poor ☐
Was it a page turner...	Good ☐	Okay ☐	Poor ☐
Was it enjoyable...	Good ☐	Okay ☐	Poor ☐
Recommend it...	Yes ☐	No ☐	

Friends who might enjoy this book...

Name: _____

My Review and Thoughts...

"Oh, magic, when a child
first knows she can read
printed words"

Betty Smith

Title: _____

Subtitle: _____

Author: _____

Genre: _____

Format: Print: ☐ E-book: ☐   # of Pages: _____

Series title: _____ # _____

Next book in series: _____

Date of purchase: _____ Date read: _____

Place of purchase: _____

I read this book: At home: ☐ Away: ☐ In transit: ☐

How would you rate this book?

Fill in mini books below 1 for poor and 5 for excellent

This book made me feel...

Happy: ☐ Sad: ☐ Angry: ☐ Warm: ☐ Disturbed: ☐

Other emotion: _____

Was the story...	Good ☐	Okay ☐	Poor ☐
Quality of writing...	Good ☐	Okay ☐	Poor ☐
Were the Characters...	Good ☐	Okay ☐	Poor ☐
Was the plot engaging...	Good ☐	Okay ☐	Poor ☐
Was it a page turner...	Good ☐	Okay ☐	Poor ☐
Was it enjoyable...	Good ☐	Okay ☐	Poor ☐
Recommend it...	Yes ☐	No ☐	

Friends who might enjoy this book...

Name: _____

My Review and Thoughts...

"To aquire the habit of reading is to construct for yourself a refuge from almost all the miseries of life."

W. Somerset Maugham

Title: _____

Subtitle: _____

Author: _____

Genre: _____

Format: Print: ☐   E-book: ☐   # of Pages: _____

Series title: _____ #_____

Next book in series: _____

Date of purchase: _____ Date read: _____

Place of purchase: _____

I read this book: At home: ☐   Away: ☐   In transit: ☐

How would you rate this book?

Fill in mini books below 1 for poor and 5 for excellent

This book made me feel...

Happy: ☐ Sad: ☐ Angry: ☐ Warm: ☐ Disturbed: ☐

Other emotion: _____

Was the story...	Good ☐	Okay ☐	Poor ☐
Quality of writing...	Good ☐	Okay ☐	Poor ☐
Were the Characters...	Good ☐	Okay ☐	Poor ☐
Was the plot engaging...	Good ☐	Okay ☐	Poor ☐
Was it a page turner...	Good ☐	Okay ☐	Poor ☐
Was it enjoyable...	Good ☐	Okay ☐	Poor ☐
Recommend it...	Yes ☐	No ☐	

Friends who might enjoy this book...

Name: _____

My Review and Thoughts...

"She reads books
as one would breathe
air, to fill up and live."
Annie Dillard

Title: _____

Subtitle: _____

Author: _____

Genre: _____

Format: Print: ☐ E-book: ☐   # of Pages: _____

Series title: _____ # _____

Next book in series: _____

Date of purchase: _____ Date read: _____

Place of purchase: _____

I read this book: At home: ☐ Away: ☐ In transit: ☐

How would you rate this book?

Fill in mini books below 1 for poor and 5 for excellent

This book made me feel...

Happy: ☐ Sad: ☐ Angry: ☐ Warm: ☐ Disturbed: ☐

Other emotion: _____

Was the story...	Good ☐	Okay ☐	Poor ☐
Quality of writing...	Good ☐	Okay ☐	Poor ☐
Were the Characters...	Good ☐	Okay ☐	Poor ☐
Was the plot engaging...	Good ☐	Okay ☐	Poor ☐
Was it a page turner...	Good ☐	Okay ☐	Poor ☐
Was it enjoyable...	Good ☐	Okay ☐	Poor ☐
Recommend it...	Yes ☐	No ☐	

Friends who might enjoy this book...

Name: _____

My Review and Thoughts...

"The one way of tolerating exsitence is to lose oneself in literature
as in a perpetual orgy."
Gustave Flaubert

Title: _____

Subtitle: _____

Author: _____

Genre: _____

Format: Print: ☐   E-book: ☐   # of Pages: _____

Series title: _____ # _____

Next book in series: _____

Date of purchase: _____ Date read: _____

Place of purchase: _____

I read this book: At home: ☐   Away: ☐   In transit: ☐

How would you rate this book?
Fill in mini books below 1 for poor and 5 for excellent

This book made me feel...
Happy: ☐ Sad: ☐ Angry: ☐ Warm: ☐ Disturbed: ☐
Other emotion: _____

Was the story...	Good ☐	Okay ☐	Poor ☐
Quality of writing...	Good ☐	Okay ☐	Poor ☐
Were the Characters...	Good ☐	Okay ☐	Poor ☐
Was the plot engaging...	Good ☐	Okay ☐	Poor ☐
Was it a page turner...	Good ☐	Okay ☐	Poor ☐
Was it enjoyable...	Good ☐	Okay ☐	Poor ☐
Recommend it...	Yes ☐	No ☐	

Friends who might enjoy this book...

Name: _____

My Review and Thoughts...

"Books are not more threatened
by Kindle than stairs
by elevators."
Stephen Fry

Title: _____

Subtitle: _____

Author: _____

Genre: _____

Format: Print: ☐   E-book: ☐   # of Pages: _____

Series title: _____ #_____

Next book in series: _____

Date of purchase: _____ Date read: _____

Place of purchase: _____

I read this book: At home: ☐   Away: ☐   In transit: ☐

How would you rate this book?
Fill in mini books below 1 for poor and 5 for excellent

This book made me feel...

Happy: ☐ Sad: ☐ Angry: ☐ Warm: ☐ Disturbed: ☐

Other emotion: _____

Was the story...	Good ☐	Okay ☐	Poor ☐
Quality of writing...	Good ☐	Okay ☐	Poor ☐
Were the Characters...	Good ☐	Okay ☐	Poor ☐
Was the plot engaging...	Good ☐	Okay ☐	Poor ☐
Was it a page turner...	Good ☐	Okay ☐	Poor ☐
Was it enjoyable...	Good ☐	Okay ☐	Poor ☐
Recommend it...	Yes ☐	No ☐	

Friends who might enjoy this book...

Name: _____

My Review and Thoughts...

"Some of the things are true and some of them are lies.
But they are all good stories."
Hilary Mantel

Title: _____

Subtitle: _____

Author: _____

Genre: _____

Format: Print: ☐   E-book: ☐   # of Pages: _____

Series title: _____ # _____

Next book in series: _____

Date of purchase: _____ Date read: _____

Place of purchase: _____

I read this book: At home: ☐   Away: ☐   In transit: ☐

How would you rate this book?
Fill in mini books below 1 for poor and 5 for excellent

This book made me feel...
Happy: ☐   Sad: ☐   Angry: ☐   Warm: ☐   Disturbed: ☐
Other emotion: _____

Was the story...	Good ☐	Okay ☐	Poor ☐
Quality of writing...	Good ☐	Okay ☐	Poor ☐
Were the Characters...	Good ☐	Okay ☐	Poor ☐
Was the plot engaging...	Good ☐	Okay ☐	Poor ☐
Was it a page turner...	Good ☐	Okay ☐	Poor ☐
Was it enjoyable...	Good ☐	Okay ☐	Poor ☐
Recommend it...	Yes ☐	No ☐	

Friends who might enjoy this book...

Name: _____

My Review and Thoughts...

"Women and fiction remain,
so far as I am concerned,
unsolved problems."

Virginia Woolf

Title: _____

Subtitle: _____

Author: _____

Genre: _____

Format: Print: ☐ E-book: ☐   # of Pages: _____

Series title: _____ # _____

Next book in series: _____

Date of purchase: _____ Date read: _____

Place of purchase: _____

I read this book: At home: ☐ Away: ☐ In transit: ☐

How would you rate this book?

Fill in mini books below 1 for poor and 5 for excellent

This book made me feel...

Happy: ☐ Sad: ☐ Angry: ☐ Warm: ☐ Disturbed: ☐

Other emotion: _____

Was the story...	Good ☐	Okay ☐	Poor ☐
Quality of writing...	Good ☐	Okay ☐	Poor ☐
Were the Characters...	Good ☐	Okay ☐	Poor ☐
Was the plot engaging...	Good ☐	Okay ☐	Poor ☐
Was it a page turner...	Good ☐	Okay ☐	Poor ☐
Was it enjoyable...	Good ☐	Okay ☐	Poor ☐
Recommend it...	Yes ☐	No ☐	

Friends who might enjoy this book...

Name: _____

My Review and Thoughts...

"If there is a book that you want to read, but it hasn't been written yet, then you must write it."
Toni Morrison

Title: _____

Subtitle: _____

Author: _____

Genre: _____

Format: Print: ☐   E-book: ☐   # of Pages: _____

Series title: _____ #_____

Next book in series: _____

Date of purchase: _____ Date read: _____

Place of purchase: _____

I read this book: At home: ☐   Away: ☐   In transit: ☐

How would you rate this book?
Fill in mini books below 1 for poor and 5 for excellent

This book made me feel...
Happy: ☐ Sad: ☐ Angry: ☐ Warm: ☐ Disturbed: ☐
Other emotion: _____

Was the story...	Good ☐	Okay ☐	Poor ☐
Quality of writing...	Good ☐	Okay ☐	Poor ☐
Were the Characters...	Good ☐	Okay ☐	Poor ☐
Was the plot engaging...	Good ☐	Okay ☐	Poor ☐
Was it a page turner...	Good ☐	Okay ☐	Poor ☐
Was it enjoyable...	Good ☐	Okay ☐	Poor ☐
Recommend it...	Yes ☐	No ☐	

Friends who might enjoy this book...

Name: _____

My Review and Thoughts...

"There is nothing
to writing. All you do is sit down
at a typewriter and bleed."
Ernest
Heningway

Title: _____

Subtitle: _____

Author: _____

Genre: _____

Format: Print: ☐   E-book: ☐   # of Pages: _____

Series title: _____ #_____

Next book in series: _____

Date of purchase: _____ Date read: _____

Place of purchase: _____

I read this book: At home: ☐   Away: ☐   In transit: ☐

How would you rate this book?

Fill in mini books below 1 for poor and 5 for excellent

This book made me feel...

Happy: ☐   Sad: ☐   Angry: ☐   Warm: ☐ Disturbed: ☐

Other emotion: _____

Was the story...	Good ☐	Okay ☐	Poor ☐
Quality of writing...	Good ☐	Okay ☐	Poor ☐
Were the Characters...	Good ☐	Okay ☐	Poor ☐
Was the plot engaging...	Good ☐	Okay ☐	Poor ☐
Was it a page turner...	Good ☐	Okay ☐	Poor ☐
Was it enjoyable...	Good ☐	Okay ☐	Poor ☐
Recommend it...	Yes ☐	No ☐	

Friends who might enjoy this book...

Name: _____

My Review and Thoughts...

"I think I may boast myself to be, with all possibile vanity, the most un-
learned and uninformed female who ever dared to be an authoress."

Jane Austen

Title: _____

Subtitle: _____
Author: _____
Genre: _____
Format: Print: ☐   E-book: ☐   # of Pages: _____
Series title: _____ # _____
Next book in series: _____
Date of purchase: _____ Date read: _____
Place of purchase: _____
I read this book: At home: ☐   Away: ☐   In transit: ☐

How would you rate this book?
Fill in mini books below 1 for poor and 5 for excellent

This book made me feel...
Happy: ☐ Sad: ☐ Angry: ☐ Warm: ☐ Disturbed: ☐
Other emotion: _____

Was the story...   Good ☐ Okay ☐ Poor ☐
Quality of writing...   Good ☐ Okay ☐ Poor ☐
Were the Characters...   Good ☐ Okay ☐ Poor ☐
Was the plot engaging...   Good ☐ Okay ☐ Poor ☐
Was it a page turner...   Good ☐ Okay ☐ Poor ☐
Was it enjoyable...   Good ☐ Okay ☐ Poor ☐
Recommend it...   Yes ☐   No ☐

Friends who might enjoy this book...

Name: _____

My Review and Thoughts...

"I was not rescued by a prince; I
was the administrator
of my own rescue."
Elizabeth
Gilbert

Title: _____

Subtitle: _____

Author: _____

Genre: _____

Format: Print: ☐ E-book: ☐   # of Pages: _____

Series title: _____ #_____

Next book in series: _____

Date of purchase: _____ Date read: _____

Place of purchase: _____

I read this book: At home: ☐ Away: ☐ In transit: ☐

How would you rate this book?
Fill in mini books below 1 for poor and 5 for excellent

This book made me feel...
Happy: ☐ Sad: ☐ Angry: ☐ Warm: ☐ Disturbed: ☐
Other emotion: _____

Was the story...	Good ☐ Okay ☐ Poor ☐
Quality of writing...	Good ☐ Okay ☐ Poor ☐
Were the Characters...	Good ☐ Okay ☐ Poor ☐
Was the plot engaging...	Good ☐ Okay ☐ Poor ☐
Was it a page turner...	Good ☐ Okay ☐ Poor ☐
Was it enjoyable...	Good ☐ Okay ☐ Poor ☐
Recommend it...	Yes ☐ No ☐

Friends who might enjoy this book...

Name: _____

My Review and Thoughts...

"Let us read and let us dance, those two amusements will never
do any harm to the world."
Voltaire

Title: _____

Subtitle: _____

Author: _____

Genre: _____

Format: Print: ☐   E-book: ☐   # of Pages: _____

Series title: _____ # _____

Next book in series: _____

Date of purchase: _____ Date read: _____

Place of purchase: _____

I read this book: At home: ☐   Away: ☐   In transit: ☐

How would you rate this book?
Fill in mini books below 1 for poor and 5 for excellent

This book made me feel...
Happy: ☐   Sad: ☐   Angry: ☐   Warm: ☐ Disturbed: ☐
Other emotion: _____

Was the story...	Good ☐	Okay ☐	Poor ☐
Quality of writing...	Good ☐	Okay ☐	Poor ☐
Were the Characters...	Good ☐	Okay ☐	Poor ☐
Was the plot engaging...	Good ☐	Okay ☐	Poor ☐
Was it a page turner...	Good ☐	Okay ☐	Poor ☐
Was it enjoyable...	Good ☐	Okay ☐	Poor ☐
Recommend it...	Yes ☐	No ☐	

Friends who might enjoy this book...

Name: _____

My Review and Thoughts...

"Writing is a splendid sorter
of...feelings, better even than
paint."

Emily Carr

Title: _____

Subtitle: _____

Author: _____

Genre: _____

Format: Print: ☐   E-book: ☐   # of Pages: _____

Series title: _____ # _____

Next book in series: _____

Date of purchase: _____ Date read: _____

Place of purchase: _____

I read this book: At home: ☐   Away: ☐   In transit: ☐

How would you rate this book?

Fill in mini books below 1 for poor and 5 for excellent

This book made me feel...

Happy: ☐   Sad: ☐   Angry: ☐   Warm: ☐   Disturbed: ☐

Other emotion: _____

Was the story...	Good ☐	Okay ☐	Poor ☐
Quality of writing...	Good ☐	Okay ☐	Poor ☐
Were the Characters...	Good ☐	Okay ☐	Poor ☐
Was the plot engaging...	Good ☐	Okay ☐	Poor ☐
Was it a page turner...	Good ☐	Okay ☐	Poor ☐
Was it enjoyable...	Good ☐	Okay ☐	Poor ☐
Recommend it...	Yes ☐	No ☐	

Friends who might enjoy this book...

Name: _____

My Review and Thoughts...

"You can never get a cup of tea large enough or a book long enough
to suit me."
C. S. Lewis

Title: _____

Subtitle: _____

Author: _____

Genre: _____

Format: Print: ☐   E-book: ☐   # of Pages: _____

Series title: _____ # _____

Next book in series: _____

Date of purchase: _____ Date read: _____

Place of purchase: _____

I read this book: At home: ☐   Away: ☐   In transit: ☐

How would you rate this book?

Fill in mini books below 1 for poor and 5 for excellent

This book made me feel...

Happy: ☐   Sad: ☐   Angry: ☐   Warm: ☐   Disturbed: ☐

Other emotion: _____

Was the story...	Good ☐	Okay ☐	Poor ☐
Quality of writing...	Good ☐	Okay ☐	Poor ☐
Were the Characters...	Good ☐	Okay ☐	Poor ☐
Was the plot engaging...	Good ☐	Okay ☐	Poor ☐
Was it a page turner...	Good ☐	Okay ☐	Poor ☐
Was it enjoyable...	Good ☐	Okay ☐	Poor ☐
Recommend it...	Yes ☐	No ☐	

Friends who might enjoy this book...

Name: _____

My Review and Thoughts...

"A book is like a vacation
for the brain."
Rachel Adams

Title: _____

Subtitle: _____

Author: _____

Genre: _____

Format: Print: ☐   E-book: ☐   # of Pages: _____

Series title: _____ # _____

Next book in series: _____

Date of purchase: _____ Date read: _____

Place of purchase: _____

I read this book: At home: ☐   Away: ☐   In transit: ☐

How would you rate this book?

Fill in mini books below 1 for poor and 5 for excellent

This book made me feel...

Happy: ☐   Sad: ☐   Angry: ☐   Warm: ☐ Disturbed: ☐

Other emotion: _____

Was the story...	Good ☐	Okay ☐	Poor ☐
Quality of writing...	Good ☐	Okay ☐	Poor ☐
Were the Characters...	Good ☐	Okay ☐	Poor ☐
Was the plot engaging...	Good ☐	Okay ☐	Poor ☐
Was it a page turner...	Good ☐	Okay ☐	Poor ☐
Was it enjoyable...	Good ☐	Okay ☐	Poor ☐
Recommend it...	Yes ☐	No ☐	

Friends who might enjoy this book...

Name: _____

My Review and Thoughts...

"The odd thing about people who had many books was how they always wanted more."
Patricia A. McKillip

Title: _____

Subtitle: _____

Author: _____

Genre: _____

Format: Print: ☐   E-book: ☐   # of Pages: _____

Series title: _____ # _____

Next book in series: _____

Date of purchase: _____ Date read: _____

Place of purchase: _____

I read this book: At home: ☐   Away: ☐   In transit: ☐

How would you rate this book?

Fill in mini books below 1 for poor and 5 for excellent

This book made me feel...

Happy: ☐ Sad: ☐ Angry: ☐ Warm: ☐ Disturbed: ☐

Other emotion: _____

Was the story...	Good ☐	Okay ☐	Poor ☐
Quality of writing...	Good ☐	Okay ☐	Poor ☐
Were the Characters...	Good ☐	Okay ☐	Poor ☐
Was the plot engaging...	Good ☐	Okay ☐	Poor ☐
Was it a page turner...	Good ☐	Okay ☐	Poor ☐
Was it enjoyable...	Good ☐	Okay ☐	Poor ☐
Recommend it...	Yes ☐	No ☐	

Friends who might enjoy this book...

Name: _____

My Review and Thoughts...

"You're never alone when
you're reading a book."
Susan Wiggs

Title: _____

Subtitle: _____

Author: _____

Genre: _____

Format: Print: ☐   E-book: ☐   # of Pages: _____

Series title: _____ # _____

Next book in series: _____

Date of purchase: _____ Date read: _____

Place of purchase: _____

I read this book: At home: ☐   Away: ☐   In transit: ☐

How would you rate this book?

Fill in mini books below 1 for poor and 5 for excellent

This book made me feel...

Happy: ☐ Sad: ☐ Angry: ☐ Warm: ☐ Disturbed: ☐

Other emotion: _____

Was the story...	Good ☐ Okay ☐ Poor ☐
Quality of writing...	Good ☐ Okay ☐ Poor ☐
Were the Characters...	Good ☐ Okay ☐ Poor ☐
Was the plot engaging...	Good ☐ Okay ☐ Poor ☐
Was it a page turner...	Good ☐ Okay ☐ Poor ☐
Was it enjoyable...	Good ☐ Okay ☐ Poor ☐
Recommend it...	Yes ☐ No ☐

Friends who might enjoy this book...

Name: _____

My Review and Thoughts...

"Let's be reasonable and add an eighth day to the week that is devoted exclusively to reading."
Lena Dunham

Title: _____

Subtitle: _____

Author: _____

Genre: _____

Format: Print: ☐   E-book: ☐   # of Pages: _____

Series title: _____ # _____

Next book in series: _____

Date of purchase: _____ Date read: _____

Place of purchase: _____

I read this book: At home: ☐   Away: ☐   In transit: ☐

How would you rate this book?

Fill in mini books below 1 for poor and 5 for excellent

This book made me feel...

Happy: ☐   Sad: ☐   Angry: ☐   Warm: ☐ Disturbed: ☐

Other emotion: _____

Was the story...	Good ☐	Okay ☐	Poor ☐
Quality of writing...	Good ☐	Okay ☐	Poor ☐
Were the Characters...	Good ☐	Okay ☐	Poor ☐
Was the plot engaging...	Good ☐	Okay ☐	Poor ☐
Was it a page turner...	Good ☐	Okay ☐	Poor ☐
Was it enjoyable...	Good ☐	Okay ☐	Poor ☐
Recommend it...	Yes ☐	No ☐	

Friends who might enjoy this book...

Name: _____

My Review and Thoughts...

"Life is too short to read
books that I'm not enjoying."
Melissa Marr

Title: _____

Subtitle: _____

Author: _____

Genre: _____

Format: Print: ☐ E-book: ☐ # of Pages: _____

Series title: _____ #_____

Next book in series: _____

Date of purchase: _____ Date read: _____

Place of purchase: _____

I read this book: At home: ☐ Away: ☐ In transit: ☐

How would you rate this book?

Fill in mini books below 1 for poor and 5 for excellent

This book made me feel...

Happy: ☐ Sad: ☐ Angry: ☐ Warm: ☐ Disturbed: ☐

Other emotion: _____

Was the story...	Good ☐	Okay ☐	Poor ☐
Quality of writing...	Good ☐	Okay ☐	Poor ☐
Were the Characters...	Good ☐	Okay ☐	Poor ☐
Was the plot engaging...	Good ☐	Okay ☐	Poor ☐
Was it a page turner...	Good ☐	Okay ☐	Poor ☐
Was it enjoyable...	Good ☐	Okay ☐	Poor ☐
Recommend it...	Yes ☐	No ☐	

Friends who might enjoy this book...

Name: _____

My Review and Thoughts...

"When her mind was discomposed...a book was the opiate that
lulled it to respond."
Ann Radcliffe

Title: _____

Subtitle: _____

Author: _____

Genre: _____

Format: Print: ☐   E-book: ☐   # of Pages: _____

Series title: _____ #_____

Next book in series: _____

Date of purchase: _____ Date read: _____

Place of purchase: _____

I read this book: At home: ☐   Away: ☐   In transit: ☐

How would you rate this book?

Fill in mini books below 1 for poor and 5 for excellent

This book made me feel...

Happy: ☐   Sad: ☐   Angry: ☐   Warm: ☐ Disturbed: ☐

Other emotion: _____

Was the story...	Good ☐	Okay ☐	Poor ☐
Quality of writing...	Good ☐	Okay ☐	Poor ☐
Were the Characters...	Good ☐	Okay ☐	Poor ☐
Was the plot engaging...	Good ☐	Okay ☐	Poor ☐
Was it a page turner...	Good ☐	Okay ☐	Poor ☐
Was it enjoyable...	Good ☐	Okay ☐	Poor ☐
Recommend it...	Yes ☐	No ☐	

Friends who might enjoy this book...

Name: _____

My Review and Thoughts...

"When we read too fast or too slowly, we understand nothing."

Blaise Pascal

Title: _____

Subtitle: _____

Author: _____

Genre: _____

Format: Print: ☐ E-book: ☐   # of Pages: _____

Series title: _____ # _____

Next book in series: _____

Date of purchase: _____ Date read: _____

Place of purchase: _____

I read this book: At home: ☐   Away: ☐   In transit: ☐

How would you rate this book?

Fill in mini books below 1 for poor and 5 for excellent

This book made me feel...

Happy: ☐   Sad: ☐   Angry: ☐   Warm: ☐ Disturbed: ☐

Other emotion: _____

Was the story...	Good ☐	Okay ☐	Poor ☐
Quality of writing...	Good ☐	Okay ☐	Poor ☐
Were the Characters...	Good ☐	Okay ☐	Poor ☐
Was the plot engaging...	Good ☐	Okay ☐	Poor ☐
Was it a page turner...	Good ☐	Okay ☐	Poor ☐
Was it enjoyable...	Good ☐	Okay ☐	Poor ☐
Recommend it...	Yes ☐	No ☐	

Friends who might enjoy this book...

Name: _____

My Review and Thoughts...

"I do not pretend to say that I was not very much pleased with him; but while I have *Udolpho* to read, I feel as if nobody could make me miserable."

Jane Austen

Title: _____

Subtitle: _____

Author: _____

Genre: _____

Format: Print: ☐ E-book: ☐ # of Pages: _____

Series title: _____ # _____

Next book in series: _____

Date of purchase: _____ Date read: _____

Place of purchase: _____

I read this book: At home: ☐ Away: ☐ In transit: ☐

How would you rate this book?

Fill in mini books below 1 for poor and 5 for excellent

This book made me feel...

Happy: ☐ Sad: ☐ Angry: ☐ Warm: ☐ Disturbed: ☐

Other emotion: _____

Was the story...	Good ☐	Okay ☐	Poor ☐
Quality of writing...	Good ☐	Okay ☐	Poor ☐
Were the Characters...	Good ☐	Okay ☐	Poor ☐
Was the plot engaging...	Good ☐	Okay ☐	Poor ☐
Was it a page turner...	Good ☐	Okay ☐	Poor ☐
Was it enjoyable...	Good ☐	Okay ☐	Poor ☐
Recommend it...	Yes ☐	No ☐	

Friends who might enjoy this book...

Name: _____

My Wish List.....

Title: _____
Author: _____
Store: _____ Library: _____
Aquired: ☐   Date: _____

Title: _____
Author: _____
Store: _____ Library: _____
Aquired: ☐   Date: _____

Title: _____
Author: _____
Store: _____ Library: _____
Aquired: ☐   Date: _____

Title: _____
Author: _____
Store: _____ Library: _____
Aquired: ☐   Date: _____

Title: _____
Author: _____
Store: _____ Library: _____
Aquired: ☐   Date: _____

Title: _____
Author: _____
Store: _____ Library: _____
Aquired: ☐   Date: _____

Notes: _____
_____
_____
_____

Title: _____
Author: _____
Store: _____ Library: _____
Aquired: ☐ Date: _____

Title: _____
Author: _____
Store: _____ Library: _____
Aquired: ☐ Date: _____

Title: _____
Author: _____
Store: _____ Library: _____
Aquired: ☐ Date: _____

Title: _____
Author: _____
Store: _____ Library: _____
Aquired: ☐ Date: _____

Title: _____
Author: _____
Store: _____ Library: _____
Aquired: ☐ Date: _____

Title: _____
Author: _____
Store: _____ Library: _____
Aquired: ☐ Date: _____

Notes: _____
_____
_____
_____
_____
_____
_____

My Personal Notes:

About the Author - Susan A. Jennings

Susan is an author, an avid reader and book collector. Tired of buying books she had already read Susan designed her own library system, documenting pertinent information related to each book and her reading habits. This *Book Tracking Journal - For Ladies Who Love to Read* is now available for all readers.

Author of many short stories, a memoir, novella and currently completeing a historical fiction trilogy. Susan writes and lives in Ottawa Canada.

Author of... *The Sackville Hotel Triliogy*

The Blue Pendant   - *Book I*
Anna's Legacy   - *Book II*   Release imminent
The Heirloom Gem - *Book III*   Release autumn 2017
Ruins in Silk   - *Prequel to The Sackville Hotel Trilogy*

Coming soon - *The Sackville Hotel Trilogy Colouring Books*
Author/designers Rosemary A. Bann & Susan A. Jennings

Susan's Short Story Series - Available at Kobo.com

Anthologies:
The Blue Heron Mysteries Book 1 and Book 2

Contributing author:
Black Lake Chronicles Volumes 1 - 5 - The Ottawa Story Spinners
Thirty at Thirty - Ottawa Independent Writers

Memoir:
Save Some for Me - A tornado lasting 20 years went through my life.
A story of spousal abuse and a single mother of five.
* *Note:* Only available in paperback on Susan's website.

All other books can be purchased from online retailers and some book stores. Details available on websites

www.susanajennings.com   susan@susanajennings.com

www.thesackvillehoteltrilogy.com

Made in the USA
Coppell, TX
03 January 2023